Jaden Smith

Gillian Gosman

PowerKiDS press.

New York

Published in 2012 by The Rosen Publishing Group, Inc.
29 East 21st Street, New York, NY 10010

First Edition

Editor: Jennifer Way
Book Design: Kate Laczynski
Layout Design: Julio Gil

Photo Credits: Cover Jason LaVeris/FilmMagic/Getty Images; p. 4 Ragnar Singsaas/WireImage/Getty Images; p. 7 Jason Merritt/Getty Images; p. 8 Eric Charbonneau/WireImage for Sony Pictures-Los Angeles/ Getty Images; p. 11 Eric Charbonneau/Le Studio/WireImage/Getty Images; p. 12 Ragnar Singsaas/Getty Images; p. 15 Chris Jackson/Getty Images; p. 16 Kevork Djansezian/Getty Images; p. 19 Larry Busacca/ Getty Images For The Recording Academy; p. 20 Jun Sato/WireImage/Getty Images.

Library of Congress Cataloging-in-Publication Data

Gosman, Gillian.
Jaden Smith / by Gillian Gosman. — 1st ed.
   p. cm. — (Kid stars!)
Includes webliography and index.
ISBN 978-1-4488-6191-0 (library binding) — ISBN 978-1-4488-6341-9 (pbk.) —
ISBN 978-1-4488-6342-6 (6-pack)
1. Smith, Jaden, 1998–—Juvenile literature. 2. Actors—United States—Biography—Juvenile literature.
I. Title. II. Series.
PN2287.S6125G67 2012
791.4302'8092—dc23
[B]

2011027671

Manufactured in the United States of America

CPSIA Compliance Information: Batch #WW12PK: For Further Information contact Rosen Publishing, New York, New York at 1-800-237-9932

Contents

Jaden Smith is a multitalented kid star. He sings, dances, and acts!

Meet Jaden Smith

It is no wonder that Jaden Smith has made a name for himself as a serious actor at such a young age. His parents are superstar actors Will Smith and Jada Pinkett Smith. His sister is pop star Willow Smith. His friends are singers, **producers**, and talent agents.

Jaden's parents may have helped the young actor get his foot in the door. He has something even more important when it comes to finding success in Hollywood and beyond, though. He has talent. Movie **critics** praise his work, and moviegoers love it, too.

Jaden Christopher Syre Smith was born on July 8, 1998, in Los Angeles, California. His father is actor, director, producer, and musician Will Smith. His mother is actress, producer, and singer Jada Pinkett Smith. His younger sister, Willow, is an actress and singer.

Jaden goes to school and does homework, just like most other kids his age. It is safe to say that his life outside of school is not ordinary, though. He makes movies, travels the world, and does **charity** work. These things are all part of the life of this kid star!

The Smith family went to the opening of *Justin Bieber: Never Say Never* together. From left to right are Jaden, Willow, Will, and Jada.

Here are Jaden and his costar and father at a special screening of *The Pursuit of Happyness*.

Jaden Finds Happyness

Jaden joined the cast of the television show *All of Us* when he was just five years old. His character, Reggie, appeared in six episodes between 2003 and 2004.

In 2006, Jaden made his first film, *The **Pursuit** of Happyness*. The movie was based on a book by Christopher Gardner, who wrote about a time in his life when he was homeless. The movie starred Jaden's real-life dad, Will Smith, as Christopher Gardner. Gardner wants to make a better life for his son, played by Jaden. Jaden was just eight years old, but movie critics agreed he was already a good actor.

A Young Actor

In 2008, Jaden was the special guest star on an episode of the Disney television comedy *The Suite Life of Zack and Cody*. Jaden played Travis, a friend of Zack and Cody's.

Jaden's next role was Jacob Benson in the 2008 movie *The Day the Earth Stood Still*. It was a **science-fiction** movie about an alien that visits Earth. The alien comes to warn humans that they must take better care of the **environment**. Jaden plays the stepson of a scientist who helps the alien and saves the human race.

The 2008 movie *The Day the Earth Stood Still* is a remake of a 1951 movie of the same name. Here is Jaden at the opening of the 2008 version.

Here is Jaden showing off some of his martial-arts moves at the opening of *The Karate Kid* in Oslo, Norway.

The Karate Kid

In 2010, Jaden played the lead role in *The Karate Kid*. In this new version, Jaden plays Dre Parker. Dre is an American boy who moves from Detroit, Michigan, to Beijing, China, when his mother gets a job there.

In China, Dre falls in love with a girl, gets bullied by an older boy, and begins to study Chinese **martial arts**. The famous martial artist Jackie Chan played the role of Dre's martial-arts teacher, Mr. Han. Jaden had to train so that he could do the martial-arts moves his character learns. Critics were impressed with Jaden's acting as well as his martial-arts skills!

Making Music

For *The Karate Kid*'s sound track, Jaden and his friend Justin Bieber recorded the song "Never Say Never." Justin sings the **verses** and chorus, while Jaden raps in the middle of the song. The song shares the movie's message that you should never give up or back down from a challenge, no matter how hard it is.

Jaden loves singing and dancing as well as acting. He has appeared in several music videos. In 2010, he danced in his sister, Willow's, video for her song "Whip My Hair."

Jaden and his sister, Willow, (left) are both interested in music. They have even sung together on stage!

Here is Jaden accepting a Nickelodeon Kid's Choice Award for Best Movie for *The Karate Kid*.

And the Winner Is . . .

Critics and fans love Jaden! For his role in *The Pursuit of Happyness*, he won a Teen Choice Award and an MTV Movie Award. For his role in *The Day the Earth Stood Still*, he won a Saturn Award for Best Younger Actor.

For his role in *The Karate Kid*, Jaden took home a Young Artists Award and a Kid's Choice Award. He was also **nominated** for an Image Award, a People's Choice Award, and a Teen Choice Award for this role. He has quickly become known in Hollywood as both a good young actor and a hard worker.

A Star's Life

Even when he is not on a movie set, Jaden stays in the spotlight. He has made guest visits to dozens of television talk shows, along with awards shows and **documentaries**. He has been a guest on *The Oprah Winfrey Show*, *The Late Show with David Letterman*, and *The View*.

In 2011, he took part in the documentary *Justin Bieber: Never Say Never*, which tells the life story of friend and fellow musician Justin Bieber. In the movie, Jaden sings on stage with Justin. This performance was filmed during Justin's concert at Madison Square Garden, in New York City.

Jaden raps in part of "Never Say Never." Here Jaden and Justin Bieber are performing the song at the Grammys in 2011.

Jaden and his sister, Willow, enjoy being youth ambassadors for Project Zambi.

Jaden lives a star's life, full of fans, fashion, and fun. His parents have taught him that being famous is a responsibility, too, though. They encourage their children to get involved in activities that make the world a better place.

Jaden and his sister, Willow, are youth **ambassadors** for Project Zambi. Project Zambi was created by the toymaker Hasbro. It gives money to care for children in Africa who have lost one or both parents to AIDS. Project Zambi has helped pay for schools, good teachers, and travel to and from school for children.

FUN FACTS

 To prepare for his role in *The Karate Kid*, Jaden practiced martial arts for 4 hours every day for three months.

 Of all of his parents' movies, Jaden's favorites are his dad's movie *I Am Legend* and his mom's movie *The Matrix Reloaded*.

 Jaden had his first on-screen kiss during the filming of *The Karate Kid*.

 Jaden was homeschooled for many years before becoming a student at the New Village Leadership Academy in Los Angeles, California.

 Jaden and Willow helped raise money for Project Zambi by signing their names on statues of elephants that were then sold on eBay.

 Jaden's Twitter account has more than 800,000 followers.

 In interviews, Jaden often jokes about his search for a girlfriend. He has not found her yet!

 In 2008, Jaden appeared in the music video for singer Alicia Keys's song "Superwoman."

 Will Smith, Jaden's dad, holds the record for winning the most Kids' Choice awards.

 While making *The Karate Kid*, Jaden injured, or hurt, his knee, but it was not a serious injury.

Glossary

ambassadors (am-BA-suh-durz) People who are the voices for countries or groups and who visit other countries or groups to share messages.

charity (CHER-uh-tee) A group that gives help to the needy.

critics (KRIH-tiks) People who write their opinions about things.

documentaries (dah-kyoo-MEN-tuh-reez) Movies or television programs about real people and events.

environment (en-VY-ern-ment) Everything that surrounds people and other living things and everything that makes it possible for them to live.

martial arts (MAR-shul ARTS) Several types of self-defense or fighting that are practiced as sport.

nominated (NO-muh-nayt-ed) Suggested that someone or something should be given an award or a position.

producers (pruh-DOO-serz) People who make movies and TV shows.

pursuit (pur-SOOT) The act of trying to get or to seek something.

science-fiction (sy-unts-FIK-shun) Work that deals with the effect of real or imagined science.

verses (VERS-ez) The parts of a song that have the same music but different words that are sung.

Index

Web Sites

Due to the changing nature of Internet links, PowerKids Press has developed an online list of Web sites related to the subject of this book. This site is updated regularly. Please use this link to access the list:
www.powerkidslinks.com/kids/smith/